Exploring
Forces and Motion

by Sasha Griffin

PEARSON
Scott
Foresman

DK

How Objects Move

Objects move in many ways. We call the act of moving **motion.**

You can push a crayon across a piece of paper in a straight line or a zigzag motion.

You can move a tennis ball up and down. A Ferris wheel moves around in a circle.

You use force to throw a ball and to make it change direction.

Force

We use **force** to move things. Force is a push or pull that makes something move.

Objects move in the direction they are pushed or pulled. When the direction of the force is changed, an object moves in a different direction.

You can make an object move faster by using more force. The merry-go-round will move faster if the boy pushes harder. It takes more force to move heavy objects than light ones.

Would the boy need to use more force to push the merry-go-round when it is empty or when it is full of kids?

Gravity

When you throw something into the air, **gravity** will pull it down. Gravity is a force that pulls things toward the center of Earth.

What do you think will happen when these children jump up? Gravity will pull them back down.

Work

When a force moves an object, we call that **work.** No work is done when an object does not move. When you pick up a pencil, you are using force and doing work.

When you push a shopping cart, you are doing work. It takes more work to push a heavy cart than to pick up a pencil. That is because you use more force to move the cart.

It takes a lot of work to move a heavy shopping cart.

A gentle kick uses little force. **A hard kick uses great force.**

Changing the Way Things Move

You use more force the farther you move an object. An object will not move very far if you push it gently. If you push it hard, it will go far.

You are doing work when you push a light object across the floor. You would do more work if you pushed a heavy object across the floor.

Friction

Friction is a force. It slows down or stops moving objects. You can skate faster on the sidewalk than on the beach. That is because friction between the wheels and the sand makes the skates slow down.

When you rub your hands together, they warm up. The friction between your hands makes heat.

Roller-skating on sand is hard!

Roller-skating on the sidewalk is easier.

Simple Machines

This axe is a wedge.

Machines are tools. They help us do work. A **simple machine** has few or no moving parts.

A wedge is a simple machine that pushes things apart. A lever is used to move things. Screws are simple machines that hold things together.

A screwdriver can be used as a lever.

A screw is a simple machine.

A bicycle has two wheels and two axles.

A wheel and axle make a simple machine. When you put force on the axle, the wheel turns too.

An inclined plane is higher at one end. It makes it easier to move things up.

A pulley is made up of a wheel and a rope. It can lift, lower, or move an object sideways.

wheel

rope

This is a pulley.

This wooden ramp is an inclined plane.

Animal Body Parts

Some animals have body parts that work like simple machines.

A woodpecker pecks holes in tree trunks. Its beak is like a wedge.

Moles have front feet that they use like levers. They move dirt as they dig.

beak

A woodpecker uses its beak like a wedge.

A mole uses its front feet like levers.

Magnets stick to a refrigerator because it is made of metal.

magnet _____

Magnets

Magnets are used in many ways. Magnets **attract** some types of metal. That means they pull some metal objects toward themselves. Magnets can push away, or **repel,** other magnets.

A magnet's force can move some objects without touching them.

A magnet has two ends, or poles. We call one end the north pole and the other the south pole. A magnet's strongest push or pull is at the poles.

Try putting two poles that are the same together. The magnets will repel each other. If you put the opposite poles together, the magnets will attract each other.

What Magnets Attract

Magnets attract objects made of iron or steel. They do not attract all kinds of metal. A magnet will attract steel paper clips. It will not attract a gold ring. Gold is a different kind of metal.

Magnets do not attract things made of wood, plastic, or paper. Do you think a magnet will attract a crayon?

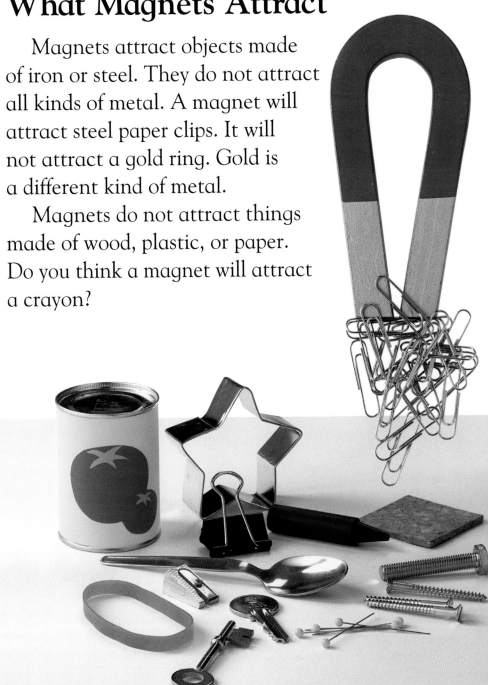

Glossary

attract	to pull toward
force	a push or pull that makes something move
friction	a force that slows or stops moving objects
gravity	a force that pulls things toward Earth's center
motion	the act of moving
repel	to push away
simple machine	a tool that has few or no moving parts
work	what happens when a force moves an object